# TO BE HONEST

## NELLE STARLING

THESE WORDS
ARE MEANT FOR YOU

# INSIDE THE HEART

i wear my heart on my sleeve even though *love* has not always been on my side, but there's something about being in the right place at the right time that keeps me on my toes despite every *heartbreak* that has landed at my feet.

that's the thing about *healing.* it is a storm cloud that follows you around for days (or weeks or months, or more) before it lets the sun touch your face. the sky is brighter now and it feels a lot like a new beginning. the kind where your legs don't feel as heavy as they did yesterday and tomorrow is something you look forward to instead of something you want to run away from. that's the beautiful thing about *forgiveness.* it has a way of showing up when you least expect it...like a long lost friend that you never thought you'd see again.

i've never met a goodbye that i liked, even the ones that were meant to be. it isn't easy, breaking yourself open and letting go of all the things that have been keeping you up at night. even though it feels like a weight has been lifted off your shoulders, you can't help but miss the pieces of yourself that you never thought would leave.

*change* looks different for everyone and i'm starting to see that with every new season, from *grief* to *happiness*, there is hope buried just under the surface waiting for you to find it. and when you do, don't forget to look back at how far you have come.

the truth is, you can turn anything into magic.

*the truth is, we all can.*

THE TRUTH ABOUT

LOVE

you deserve a shout it from the rooftops kind of
love. a slow kind of love. a dance in the middle
of the street under the stars kind of love, an i will
catch you if you fall kind of love. a shoulder to cry
on kind of love. a flowers just because kind of love.
an if you hurt, i hurt, kind of love. a dream come
true kind of love. an i'm sorry i was wrong kind of
love.

anything less is not worth your time.
anything less does not deserve to hold your heart.

i hope you know that
you are everything i could ever need
on the good days and the bad.
you give me a reason to look forward to tomorrow
when stepping one foot in front of the other feels
impossible.

thank you for reaching for my hand
when i am lost and for holding my head high
when i feel like giving up.

my eyes can see the sun because of you
and i hope i'm able to give you as much light
as you have given me.

my head:
*i don't think this is a good idea.*

my heart:
*but what if it is?*

letting go means you loved yourself more
than to keep holding on to something that hurt
more than it didn't.

*putting yourself first is never a failure*

if i smile while i'm sleeping
it's because i'm dreaming of you.

what you should know about me is that i will love
you through every season. i am the kind of person
who will help you bury your worries under the
snow and dig them back up when you're ready
to face them again. i will plant seeds in all of the
places it hurts because flowers help make anything
better and spring is just around the corner waiting
to show you that hope still lives here. maybe it's
true that when it rains it pours, but that just means
there will be a rainbow on the horizon ready for
you to see it. and if you start to fall, you can lean
in my direction because i promise i'm not going
anywhere unless it's with you.

you held my hand while i fixed myself
and i'll never forget the way that made me feel.

*when they let you be the hero*

love yourself when things are hard, when you make mistakes, when you give up before trying, when you don't workout for the second day in a row, when you lay in bed all day, when all you feel is sadness, when a promise is hard to keep, when you don't know what to say, when you say too much, when you fail, when you don't want to.

*love yourself even when you don't feel like it*

my smile is different now. you gave it a reason to
show up after so many years of hiding and i still
don't know what to do with all these feelings. i found
a home in your arms and forever under the stars,
because like them, you are always there, giving me a
reason to believe that wishes can come true.

you and i were everything each other needed,
but you didn't know how to see me
while you were still trying to find yourself
(and that is devastatingly okay).

*when it's the right person, but the wrong lifetime*

they say love is invisible,
but when i look in the mirror
i know that isn't true.

*self love*

*repeat after me:*

loving them shouldn't hurt.

i thought a love like ours would last a lifetime.
it was a happily ever after kind of love.
the kind where our laugh started to sound the
same and we knew each other by heart,
but somewhere along the way that wasn't enough
to keep love on our side.

where did we go wrong
when everything felt so right?

yesterday feels so far away now
and i don't know if i'll ever be able
to wake up tomorrow and not miss you.

i will take my time loving you,
because what i know for sure
is that i want this to last forever.

THE TRUTH ABOUT

# HEARTBREAK

i need to learn how to stop looking for a love
that doesn't know how to find me.

*i don't want what doesn't want me*

sometimes,
i can still feel you next to me.
i can still smell you on my clothes
even though they've been washed.
i can still hear the front door unlock
at 5:30 when you get home from work.
i can still see you when i close my eyes.

forgetting is so hard
when remembering is so easy.

today i reached out to your side of the bed
even though i knew you weren't there—
maybe it's muscle memory
or maybe it's the hopeful part of me that thinks
you will come back while i'm sleeping
even though you've been gone for months.

i break my own heart loving you,
but no matter how hard i try to leave that part of
me behind, i keep looking for you in the people i
meet hoping that i'll find you again someday.

maybe in another lifetime
i will find you again
and it will be different.

you: *i don't feel the same way anymore.*

me: *i don't know how i could ever stop.*

people come and go
and i don't think my heart
will ever be okay
with this.

*why does everything have a beginning and an end*

the truth is,
i don't talk about it anymore,
but that doesn't mean it stopped hurting.

maybe one day i can go to sleep
knowing that i have something to look forward to
tomorrow.

*maybe one day i'll stop waiting for you*

everyone keeps saying that
it won't hurt like this forever,
but that's what i'm afraid of.
what will be left of us after the hurting stops
besides a box of memories under the bed
and trying to remember what it sounds like
when you say my name.

remembering—
that's the part that hurts the most
when all you want is to forget the thing
that used to make you happy.

the sad thing about forever is that i believed
it could happen to us.

i thought you were my perfect timing.
my everything feels too right to be wrong.
my if you jump, i jump.
my light in the middle of the dark.
my hug at the end of a bad day.
my i'll love you forever.

you were my everything,
but you didn't know how to let me be yours.

i think i've been hurt too many times
to still believe in love.

*how do you fix something that's already broken*

it's okay if you asked them to stay—
we were made to do whatever it takes to survive
and when the person you've given your heart to
shows you that they are going to break it,
it feels like every part of you is about to die.

asking them not to leave doesn't mean you are weak.
it means you'll do anything to stay alive.

THE TRUTH ABOUT

# HEALING

*things to remember about healing from something*

everything hurts before it gets better.

you have to leave some things behind.

you are so much stronger than what you fear.

it's okay to be sad and not have the energy to hide it.

you won't heal if you keep touching where it hurts.

don't forget to love the parts of yourself that are still learning.

i will keep growing
until the sun gives me a reason
to stop believing that i can.

*the light never goes out*

everything is changing
and maybe that means you don't know
where you're going,
but maybe that means something beautiful
is just around the corner.

one day you will wake up and your mornings won't feel as heavy. the birds will sound beautiful again and the sun will rise as it always has, but this time you won't hide your face under the pillows and ask it to leave. you won't skip breakfast (or lunch or dinner) and you'll take a shower, brush your hair and get dressed because today isn't as hard as it was yesterday or the day before. time will pass by faster because you'll stop checking your phone for their name wondering if they miss you, too. then you will turn on the music and instead of crying in the middle of the living room floor, you will dance your heart out and call it therapy.

*when healing finally finds you*

give yourself permission to move forward,
(but only when you are ready).

it's okay to heal
even if they don't tell you
they're sorry.

i've always wanted to be the kind of person
that gets it right on the first try.
the kind of person that follows their heart
to forever with no fear of it breaking
before it gets to the good part.

but that's the thing about love,
you don't get to decide who stays.

so don't leave yourself behind
waiting for someone to change how they feel
about you when you still haven't met all of the
people who will know how to love you back.

you will never find yourself
if you keep pointing the light
in the wrong direction.

sometimes i wonder how you're doing. i wonder if
you found the happiness that you couldn't find with
me. i stopped losing sleep awhile ago, but there are
these things i like to call *gentle reminders* that keep me
from forgetting. some days i can hear you singing in
the shower and i still catch myself making your coffee
in the morning.

what i really mean is,
i hope that you're somewhere out there remembering
the good days. i hope that if you think of me you still
smile even if i wasn't your first choice. i hope you
know i never wanted us to end. i hope you know it's
okay that we did.

that's the thing about nostalgia,
it takes you back to a time in your life
that you walked away from,
but it reminds you of all the reasons
you wanted to stay.

i'm tired of hurting on the inside and hiding it
on the outside.

i'm tired of pretending that everything is okay
to protect your feelings.

i'm tired of fighting to get through the day
only to wake up and have to do it all over again.

i'm tired of wishing time away
when there is still so much i have left to see.

i'm tired of losing hope in myself
and humanity.

i'm tired of having to heal from the damage
that other people have caused.

i'm tired of being
me.

there you are,
smiling in pictures like you forgot about me so
quickly.

here i am,
waiting for my heart to stop breaking,
wondering when it will be my turn to forget, too.

*you always make things look so easy*

never apologize for the way you put yourself
back together after they broke you.

it's okay if you don't smile when it hurts.

how can you heal if you keep pretending
that everything is okay?

<u>*the parts about healing no one talks about*</u>

the wound is how the light gets in.

you won't forget the ones who leave
when a heart was made to remember.

you don't stop feeling it
just because it isn't there.

your story will keep going.

THE TRUTH ABOUT

# FORGIVENESS

*OPTION A:* continue holding on to anger.

*OPTION B:* pretend that you don't care anymore and smile like you mean it.

*OPTION C:* honor your feelings. be honest with yourself. let go when it gets too heavy. forgive when the time is right.

when they ask me about you
i still smile because the stories
that i have to tell are just as beautiful
today as they were when you were still
holding my hand.

i remember your laugh, but mostly
i remember the sound of mine because it was
honest.

it was so easy loving you
and maybe when they ask about me,
you'll remember why it was so easy
to love me back.

it's true what they say—
not all stories have a happy ending,
but ours had a happy middle and beginning
and that will always be enough
because it means that we are a story
worth remembering.

thank you for breaking my heart in all the right places so that the light could find me.

*i forgive you*

*do you want to know the truth?*

it's going to be a hard pill to swallow. accepting that you loved them with all of your heart and it wasn't enough, but always remember that you deserve so much more than a one sided love story. time will pass slowly in the beginning and you will try to hold on to every piece of them...the sound of their voice, their sweatshirt that you wore to bed at night, the smell of them on your pillow.

eventually the hurting won't feel the same and you'll understand why loving them wasn't enough to make them stay (and why it's better that they didn't).

and then when you least expect it, you will find forgiveness waiting for you to pick it up off the ground and you will hold onto it knowing that everything is different, but you are exactly where you are meant to be.

*a simple truth:*

love will never leave you hungry
and forgiveness will always feed you.

in the end, i wanted it to be you,
but some people are a lesson to learn from
instead of someone that you get to keep.

*a gentle reminder:*

growing will be painful.
it will stretch you in every direction and make you
feel like you are about to break, but really this is
change letting you know that something beautiful is
about to happen.

healing can also feel like loss,
but your heart will remind you when it isn't.

forgiveness is for you, not for them.

be who you need.

don't let anyone make you believe that *feeling too
much* or being *too emotional* is anything less than a
superpower.

i learned to stop saying sorry
for things that were not my fault.

i will keep trying
until i learn how to get it right.

*it's okay if it takes longer than you thought it would*

every version of yourself
deserves forgiveness.

no one falls in love with someone
thinking that they will become a stranger.

*i believed i would know you forever*

*i hope that forgiving me isn't the hardest
thing anyone has to do.*

maybe if i hide my loneliness,
you won't see it and neither will i.

*you took my heart with you when you left*

i will keep finding ways to look on the bright side
until i learn how to love every part of myself
down to the shadows at my feet.

*i'm sorry for all of the mean things i said to me*

THE TRUTH ABOUT

# CHANGE

the truth is
i don't know where i'm going,
but when i get there
i know it will be beautiful.

no matter how much you change,
you will never forget where you came from
and you'll always remember why you left.

*there's a reason why saying goodbye*
*is so much harder than hello*

i let go because you shouldn't have to work so hard
for something that is meant to be. i always had a
fear that life would divide us, but in the end it was
us that didn't know how to keep it together. i guess
love isn't enough when everything else shows up,
too.

i won't forget when everything felt right
and i will remember the way we were
before it all changed.

*sometimes i wonder*
*am i free or am i lonely*

i can't help but wonder if this version of myself is
one that will make them want to stay or leave.

the thing about change is that
it can rip you open one second
and set you free the next.

trust the process and remember that
there is a reason you left something behind.

*your future needs you*
*more than your past does*

*what you see:*

is me, pretending that
everything is okay.

*what you don't see:*

is me, stuck in between waiting and forgetting,
wondering if *see you later* was really *goodbye*.

*note to self:*

don't break your own rules for anyone.

it's okay if you outgrow them.

don't bend yourself to fit into their world
when they didn't show up to be part of yours.

you are so much more than second best.

they will never know how you feel
if you don't tell them.

it was hard work,
trying to make myself fit into a box that you
wanted to hold, but then i opened my eyes and
realized that my dreams were too big for a closed
mind like yours.

*never shrink yourself to make them love you*

i wish i could stop missing
all of the past versions of people
i used to love.

the beautiful thing is that
the birds keep singing
even when the seasons change.

the truth is,
it hurts right before
it's about to change you.

i remember that days with you
were when i was the happiest.
my smile reached to my ears
and my heart was living on cloud nine.
there was something about the way your hands
fit perfectly in my back pockets.
the way you brought me back to earth.

i still believe that you and i were made for each other,
but as the days pass by like a slow moving train,
i've learned to accept that forever wasn't meant for
us in this life, but i hope in the next one we will know
how to get it right.

and what a beautiful thing it is,
watching you come back to life
after you thought you never could.

i'll never forget the day i met you.
you became the main character in my story
and sometimes i still wonder if you might
find your way back again.
i was a hopeless romantic and you...
you were my right place at the right time,
my dream come true, my easiest hello and my
hardest goodbye.

but what you should know is that i'm so glad
you showed up when you did. you and i were the
chapter i didn't know i needed and so many of
the pages are folded at the corners because i know
i will want to go back so i can always remember
how good it was.

the sad truth is, we couldn't keep each other
forever, but i think it's because we both knew
there were other people who needed us more
in this lifetime.

THE TRUTH ABOUT

GRIEF

missing you is like a thunderstorm. it is loud, heavy
and sometimes unexpected. everything around me
is turning gray because i don't remember how to see
in color. i look out the window and wonder when it
will stop.

*all this hurting. all this grief. all this darkness.*

the truth is,
i don't think the rain is leaving anytime soon.

the truth is,
i will miss you even when the power comes back on.

sometimes the hardest part is knowing that
we will never have enough time with each other.

*it will always be too soon to lose you*

at the end of the day
i just miss having someone to love,
but i lost myself trying to keep you
when you were already saying goodbye.

i hold on to the past
so i can keep running into you.

*i hope you never forget everything i'll always remember*

sometimes i'm afraid to heal because i fear that healing will bring me closer to forgetting. i do not want to grow further away from you because at least missing you still means a part of you is close to me.

*grief doesn't mean it's the end*
*and healing doesn't mean it is either*

somewhere along the way
you learn to make room for grief
because it's something that never leaves you.

*when you ask me if it still hurts*
*i think it always will*

when i close my eyes, i smile
because i know that i'll still see you again.

some days are harder than others and i've been
living with this ache buried in my chest since you
left, but how different would life be if i didn't have
you to miss?

without you i can barely breathe,
but knowing you is the reason i can.

does it stop hurting
if you can't see it?

*i hope so*

it's a different kind of grief
when the person you miss is still alive.
when they are just a phone call away.
when you can still text them in the morning
and before you go to sleep at night.
when you can drive 15 minutes to your favorite
coffee shop and meet at the park bench for lunch.

isn't it torture?
this choice to keep missing them
and holding on to hope that maybe
they miss you, too.

i hope your heart is a little less heavy today.

i hope when your feet touch the ground you're not
afraid to fall, because even if you do, getting up
will be something worth celebrating.

i hope you know it's okay if things get messy and
stay that way for awhile. even flowers grow through
the cracks of concrete and still look beautiful.

i hope you remember to love yourself through the
heartache. it will start to feel better when you're
ready to believe that it can.

but who will i call
when something good happens?

*happiness isn't the same without you here*

the truth is,
yesterday i cried. i cried in the kitchen making
breakfast and while i folded the laundry. i cried in
the car waiting in the drive thru because i thought
ice cream would make it all better, but sometimes
that isn't true. i cried in the shower because then no
one would notice that i wasn't okay.

the truth is,
today i smiled and i surprised myself. i almost
forgot what it felt like to be this close to happiness.

the truth is,
tomorrow is a new day and it has the potential to be
one of the best days of your life, but even if it's not,
just remember that a bad day is still only 24 hours.

*things i think about when i can't sleep*

why does it still hurt if i'm healing?

i wish i was someone that you didn't want to lose.

you should be here.

i need to show up for myself.

maybe it's not too late.

i think it's too late.

when i thought about telling you
how much i miss you,
i realized that wouldn't be fair
to either one of us.

THE TRUTH ABOUT

# HAPPINESS

## POV

i am laying next to you as we start to fall asleep
and my heart is happy because it knows that i'm
finally kissing the right person goodnight.

it took awhile to get here,
but now i understand why happiness
is impossible to hide once you've found
that there are so many reasons
to smile.

i pray that someday
we will meet each other again
for the first time.

*i hope next time we won't be an almost*

*something to remember:*

one day you will have everything you prayed for.

i will never regret the way i fought
for our love story.
and i will never regret the way i put myself first
when you didn't fight for the same.

*waiting to be loved is the loneliest thing in the world*

to the girl i used to be...

we made it to the other side of healing.
we smile again and it's honest.
we let go and it didn't break us.
we laugh until we cry (and it doesn't hurt).
we like who we're becoming.
we learned how to love ourself again.
we found something worth waking up for.
we stayed.

you can't catch up to someone
who doesn't want to walk beside you.

*never forget to chase your dreams instead of people*

*i hope you know that...*

it's impossible to carry everything at once.
set things down if it gets too heavy.

it's okay if you need to take a break from being
the listener and the healer.

you can have empathy and boundaries
at the same time.

your feelings are not wrong.

you are the writer of your story and you don't have
to read it out loud if you don't want to.

your happiness is sacred. don't give yourself away
to people who don't know how to care for you.

i promise that the sun is shining
even if you can't feel it.

i gave you my heart
because i knew
that it didn't belong
anywhere else.

*things i wish i said*
please stay a little longer.

*things i wish you said*
i'm not ready to say goodbye.

if i've learned anything in this life
it's that you should never hold back.

tell them how you feel.

if you like something about someone,
give them the compliment - it may be the nicest
thing they've heard in awhile.

say the words before you run out of time
because you are one day closer to too late.

this is a reminder to slow down. enjoy the moment. open your eyes. follow your heart. live every minute with intention and purpose. listen to the music. dance your heart out. be present for the late night conversations. eat the ice cream sundae (and the cookies), be whoever makes you happy. wear whatever you want. make mistakes and learn from them. surround yourself with good people. stay curious. ask questions. take your time.

*don't rush through your day just to get to tomorrow*
*there is so much that you will miss*

*and my heart said*

this love was planted here for a reason

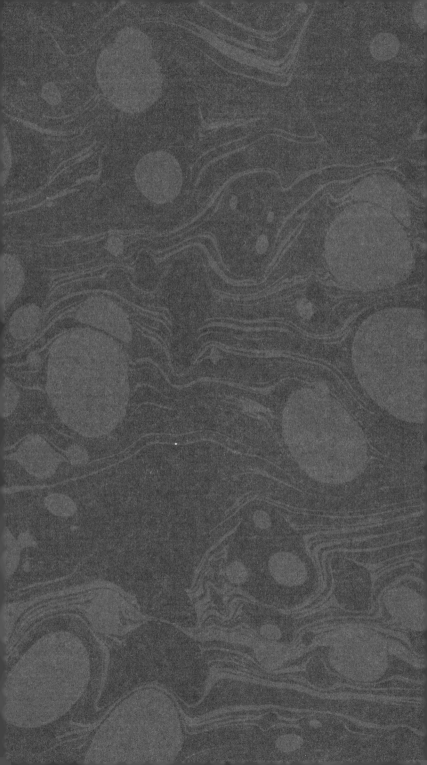

*I write because then it stops hurting*

*follow along on:*
*Instagram @nellestarlingpoetry*
*TikTok @thesewordsaremeantforyou*

*To Be Honest* © 2023 by Nelle Starling
ISBN: 9798366970464
Cover design & book design: Nelle Starling
Illustrations obtained via creative commons license

*i hope this good dream never ends*